Captain
Manoj Kumar Pandey

Full Name : Manoj Kumar Pandey

Date of Birth : June 25, 1975

Birthplace : Rudha Village,
District Sitapur,
Uttar Pradesh

Martyrdom : July 3, 1999

Parents : Smt Mohini Pandey,
Sh Gopi Chand Pandey

Service : The Indian Army

Rank : Captain

Unit : 1/11 Gorkha Rifles

War : Kargil War (Operation Vijay – 1999)

Award : Param Vir Chakra (Posthumously)

Special Recognition : Manoj Kumar Pandey stood with all his courage at his post 'Pehalwan Chowki' (in Khalubar area) at the height of 19,700 feet for a long time and carried out his duty with absolute courage and dedication.

MANOJ KUMAR
PANDEY

The exuberant words, *"I swear that I will even defeat death if it comes in the way of my duty"*, were of martyr Captain Manoj Kumar Pandey, the hero of the Kargil war. He was one such daredevil of the Kargil war who wrote a new chapter of patriotism with his combat skills and passion for the country. Despite being severely wounded by enemy bullets, he had his fingers gripped on his gun firmly. He kept encouraging his fellow soldiers to complete their mission and overpowered the enemy weapons with his bravery.

Early Years

Manoj Kumar Pandey was born on June 25, 1975 in the Rudha Village of Sitapur District in Uttar Pradesh. His father Sh Gopi Chand Pandey and mother Smt Mohini Pandey raised him with the tradition of valour since childhood, which later became the foundation of his life. Born in an ordinary middle class family, Manoj had prodigious intelligence since childhood. After completing his 6th standard in Rani Laxmibai Vidyalaya, Lucknow, Manoj was enrolled in the Sainik School in Lucknow. This laid the foundation for him to join the Army. Though Manoj had his main inspiration from a TV serial 'Param Vir Chakra' that he watched as a child, enrolling in the Army School gave direction and flight to his dreams. In the meantime, he also learned the art of leadership, which is mandatory to become military officer. Manoj attained knowledge of each and every such discipline in the military school that proved useful for him to become a military officer. This was also the reason that he qualified for the National

Khalubar

Defence Academy (NDA) exam in his very first attempt. He was interviewed through the Service Selection Board (SSB), Varanasi. In this interview he was asked a question, “Why do you want to join the Indian Army”. In response to this question he immediately replied, "I want to win the Param Vir Chakra”. The officers present in the interview board were astonished by his reply. They told Manoj that the award is usually honoured posthumously. On this Manoj proudly replied that, "I am always ready to sacrifice my life for my country". True to his words, Captain Manoj Kumar Pandey did win the country’s highest gallantry award but unfortunately did not live to receive it in person. After commissioning he got posted in Kashmir Valley and thereafter he was moved to Siachen. Whilst in Siachen he received orders to move to Batalik Sector, where the first intrusions by the Pakistani Army were detected.

Kargil War

On May 3, 1999, a Buddhist shepherd, Tashi Namgyal, noticed some unusual movement in the valley. He informed the Indian Army and upon detailed investigation, it was found that the Pakistani Army had infiltrated at 150 posts of the Indian Army along 160-kilometre-long Line of Control (LOC). Till that year it was an unsigned pact between both the countries to not man the border posts during the winter season as the temperature in these regions goes below till minus 40 to 50 degree Celsius. In such harsh climatic conditions, it doesn't

make any sense to deploy troops. But, unfortunately Pakistan betrayed our trust and sent intruders with the ill intention to secure the unmanned posts on the Indian side.

After all, why were these high peaks of Kargil so crucial? It is because, India's National Highway 1-D is just 8 kilometres away from the Line of Control (LOC). From these peaks Pakistan can have direct control of the Dras-Leh road, which goes upward in the north till Siachen. Cutting off these critical areas from India and eventually establishing its supremacy could be a game changer for Pakistani Army. Initially, India thought that the infiltrators were just a handful of armed terrorists but this assessment turned out to be completely erroneous. The attackers were none other than disguised Pakistani soldiers who sneaked into the Indian territory, faking as intruders.

Pakistani soldiers were sitting at a substantial height in extreme cold conditions having strong fortifications with abundant food and water supply at their disposal. Since, they had settled there with proper arrangements to face the extreme weather conditions, they became acclimatized and comfortable with the prevailing weather. Also, they were well equipped with heavy artillery and ammunition.

It is said that the enemy sitting at a higher point is far more powerful than the enemy below. So much so, that even if a stone is thrown from a hill, it hits the ground like a bullet. Therefore, considering the situation the Indian Army deployed its soldiers on

the entire battlefield in a ratio of 16:1. It means 16 Indian soldiers deployed for each Pakistani soldier.

One of the main centres of the Kargil war was a place known as 'Dras'. It is the second coldest inhabited place in the world. Even the temperature in this region went down to 54 degrees below zero. Due to such harsh climatic conditions 'Dras' is also called as the Siberia of India.

The height of these peaks, where the Kargil War was actually fought, goes up to 16000 feet. No battle has ever been fought in the world at such heights. Amidst icy winds on the bare mountains there were hardly any place to hide behind. It was a clear climb on the hill in the direct line of fire from the enemy. Nonetheless, probably these brave Indian soldiers are moulded to face any unprecedented situation. Even these adverse circumstances could not shake the indomitable fighting spirit of our soldiers.

The Kargil area was mainly divided into six sectors:

1. Dras Sector
2. Mushkoh Sector
3. Kaksar Sector
4. Kargil Sector
5. Batalik Sector
6. Turtuk Sector

In the early days of May 1999, it took some time for our Army to understand and assess the seriousness of the situation. On May 26,

1999 the Indian Army launched Operation 'Vijay' and the Indian Air Force launched Operation 'Safed Sagar' to counter the intrusion.

Finally, by the month of July 1999, our brave hearts freed every inch of our land from the enemy's hold. Five hundred and twenty seven (527) brave soldiers sacrificed their lives to win this war, showing great courage, valour and bravery. Their names will be engraved in the history of Indian Armed Forces forever.

Role of Captain Manoj Kumar Pandey in War

By the end of June 1999, our soldiers were gaining confidence to defeat the Pakistani Army. Still several challenges were there to be overcome. In July 2007, when I travelled to Kargil from Leh, a soldier present in my vehicle stopped it at a place in Batalik. The river Indus enters the Pakistan territory from this region. The scenic beauty of high mountains was a sight to behold. The soldier informed us that at this place Captain Manoj Kumar Pandey had sacrificed his life for the country. The mountains of Batalik were bound to remind everyone of the supreme sacrifice of Captain Pandey. The Kukarthang, Juber and Khalubar areas of Batalik are extremely difficult as compared to the peaks of Dras and Kargil.

It was May 3, 1999 when the news of intrusion was reported from Garkhon area of Batalik sector. The infiltration was confirmed in the next four-five days and the Indian Army immediately swung into action. 1/11 Gorkha Regiment had almost completed its tenure

in Siachen and Captain Manoj was about to proceed on leave when the Regiment received the orders to reach Batalik. Being deployed in Siachen region 1/11 Gorkha Regiment did not need acclimatization. The Gorkha Regiment has a special place in the Indian war history. With their indomitable courage and bravery, the Gorkhas have the expertise to turn the tables around.

On June 30, 1999 the 22 Grenadiers had attacked 'Khalubar' in the Batalik sector. They gained some success there. Then the first Regiment of 11 Gorkha Rifles was deployed there on July 2, 1999. There is an area known as 'Bunker Area', which is below the two peaks of Khalubar South and Khalubar North. Captain Manoj Pandey was sent to hoist the victory flag in this area. It was four o'clock in the morning and it was very cold. Nevertheless, the Gorkha soldiers of Captain Manoj's Regiment were all set to kill or die. Captain Manoj assessed the situation and found that there were a total of six enemy bunkers in that area that were to be destroyed. He called for Havildar Bhim Bahadur and ordered him to destroy two bunkers on his right hand side and decided to destroy four bunkers on his left hand side by himself. As soon as the deafening war cry of 'Jai Mahakali, Aayo Gurkhali' echoed in the sky, the Gorkha soldiers felt the surge of heat in their blood. The end of enemies seemed definite that day. Manoj began to move forward. Destroying the first bunker, he killed two Pakistani soldiers. Similarly, he killed two more Pakistani soldiers while destroying the second bunker. However, he was hit by some

enemy bullets in his leg and shoulder by the time he launched his attack on the third bunker. Nevertheless, he kept his courage intact and attacked the fourth enemy bunker with hand grenades. Meanwhile, a shot fired from the Universal Machine Gun (UMG) hit Captain Manoj on his face and this braveheart attained martyrdom for his country. Before sacrificing his life for our motherland, Manoj's last words were, "Chhodnu Nahin", which in Nepali means 'don't leave the enemy'. Bravehearts like Captain Manoj are rarely born. Our Army had occupied the entire bunker area by 5 pm on July 3, 1999. Captain Manoj was awarded the 'Param Vir Chakra' and Havildar Bhim Bahadur was awarded the 'Vir Chakra' for displaying exceptional gallantry in the battlefield. Captain Manoj Kumar Pandey has adhered to the highest tradition of the Indian Army by sacrificing his life for the country. We Indians will always remember his bravery and valour.

Children, you should not only read and know about this great heroic story of our brave soldiers, but also share it with your friends, parents and siblings, so that we never lose sight of what these heroes did for our nation. Captain **Manoj Kumar Pandey** is a true inspiration for all of us as he sacrificed his life for our country. He displayed unflinching confidence, valour and bravery in the Kargil war. Our country will always be grateful to its hero.

❑❑❑

MANOJ KUMAR
PANDEY